PRAISE FOR THE SMART THINKING BOOK

"Short, direct and powerful."
Seth Godin, Author

"It's crisply written and very clear. Just what marketing and business students need."
Dave Trott, Author *Predatory Thinking*

"When you want to take your mind for a sprint, pack *The Smart Thinking Book* as your protein bar."
Richard Hytner, Deputy Chairman, Saatchi & Saatchi Worldwide, and author of *Consiglieri*

"A fast, no bullshit shot in the arm for all of us who forget how simple business can be. Punchy + Bouncy = Refreshing!"
Chris Baréz-Brown, Founder of Upping Your Elvis, and author of *Shine* and *Free!*

"So many business books comprise a few good ideas and a lot of padding. Kevin's book is full of a lot of good ideas and NO padding. Which would you prefer?"
Euan Semple, ex-BBC, and author of *Organizations Don't Tweet, People Do*

"I like my fiction meandering and time consuming. I like my non-fiction informative and straight to the point. Kevin's book meets the second criteria admirably – simple valuable messages, efficiently conveyed."
George Cooper, author *Money, Blood and Revolution*

"Another gem from the King of Common Sense. Kevin has beautifully captured the most common challenges that we all encounter in our business lives, and distilled them down to their most fundamental parts, and offered a variety of possible solutions. Invaluable and inspirational."
Chris Carmichael, Global Head of Media, HSBC

TO:

ROSANNA, SHAUNAGH,

AND SARAH

Thanks for comment on the early draft:
Chris Barez-Brown, Chris Carmichael, Katy Clarkson,
George Cooper, Rosie Duncan, Seth Godin, Richard Hytner,
Euan Semple, Rory Sutherland, Dawn Sillett and Dave Trott.

Thanks to my wife Sarah
for helping me plan the book on the wall.

Thanks to Jim Collins and Seth Godin
for their words of encouragement.

THE
SMART
THINKING
BOOK

60 BURSTS

OF BUSINESS BRILLIANCE

KEVIN DUNCAN

LONDON   NEW YORK   BOGOTA
MADRID   BARCELONA   BUENOS AIRES
MEXICO CITY   MONTERREY   SAN FRANCISCO
                SHANGHAI

Published by
LID Publishing Ltd
One Mercer Street, Covent Garden,
London, WC2H 9JQ

31 West 34th Street, Suite 7004,
New York, NY 10001, US

info@lidpublishing.com
www.lidpublishing.com

A member of:

BPR
Business Publishers Roundtable

www.businesspublishersroundtable.com

Printed in the Czech Republic by Finidr

ISBN: 978-1-910649-21-3

Cover and page design: Laura Hawkins

CONTENTS

INTRODUCTION

A lot of people have been very responsive to *The Diagrams Book* and *The Ideas Book*.

With everyone so frantically busy, many are grateful for books that allow them to pick up intelligent ideas fast.

So I have been writing shorter and shorter.

Some of the most inspiring thoughts I have come across are gathered here in *The Smart Thinking Book*.

In this format, I have drawn together 60 bursts of business intelligence.

You can read the whole thing in an hour, or each thought in one minute.

Each provocation is ideal for sticking on the wall, scrutinizing fast with some colleagues (or on your own), and working out how to galvanize your business or project with a new angle.

Good luck applying them to your work, and do let me know how you get on with these ideas.

Kevin Duncan, Westminster 2015

INNOVATION

CREATIVITY

RELATIONSHIPS

THINKING

A plan is just a plan. Just because it is written down, it doesn't mean that's what is going to happen.

"No battle plan survives contact with the enemy," according to Colin Powell, the former US Secretary of State.

In other words, planning is theoretical.

And there's a lot of difference between theory and practice.

Mike Tyson had a more blunt way of putting it. "Everybody has a plan until they get punched in the face."

Everything changes all the time. So the bulk of assumptions made at the planning stage may well be wrong.

In fact, they usually are.

"A good plan violently executed now is better than a perfect plan executed next week," said the famous military commander George S. Patton.

So the best approach is to draw up a reasonable plan, fast, and then get on with it.

According to statistician George Box,
"All models are wrong, but some are useful."

A model is just a representation.

Models are usually simplified, often to the point
of being simplistic.

As mathematician Alfred North Whitehead said:
"Seek simplicity and distrust it."

Many business people make the mistake of
assuming that the model they have drawn up is
how reality will turn out.

It isn't.

It's just a guide. A suggestion. A shape.

So next time you are presented with a model,
challenge it.

And next time you are designing one,
don't necessarily believe it.

A target is just a target.

It's something to aim at, but you might not hit it.

A percentage is just a percentage.
A percentage of what?

1% of a lot might be a lot. 99% of not very
much might be... not very much.

So arbitrarily adding 10% to last year's target
may well be pointless.

There is absolute performance, and there is
relative performance.

Absolute performance is what *you* want to achieve.

Relative performance compares yours with
the competition.

Do you really care what *they* do?

Or would you rather concentrate on your own
intentions and aspirations?

By all means set targets, but do it on your
own terms.

Direction is a line or a course.

It goes a certain way.

It's not the same as the destination.

Barely any journey, whether physical or temporal, follows a single straight line.

Most involve a number of directions, plural.

So your direction today may well be different from your direction tomorrow, even though the destination remains the same.

Smart business people understand that many directions are needed to reach the ultimate destination.

Don't confuse the two.

Just because a lot is going on it doesn't mean that you are actually getting anywhere.

Some people, and businesses generally, love having lots of people rushing around.

It makes them feel productive.

Regardless of what they are doing, all the frenetic activity suggests that much helpful work is being done.

People even say sometimes that they like the buzz.

But it's a bit like a goalkeeper diving to save a penalty.

He might be just as effective staying exactly where he is.

So movement doesn't necessarily mean progress.

Don't confuse the two.

You need to be doing the *right* things.

It is good to have a clear point of view.

If you aspire to being an effective manager, this is precisely what's needed.

It rallies staff around a cause, and explains what you are trying to do.

But things rarely go exactly as planned.

New information emerges all the time.

So the smart leader needs to realize when to change.

It's painful to watch someone who is wedded to an approach and won't adjust.

Circumstances have changed, but they won't.

They stubbornly stick to the original plan.

As the economist John Maynard Keynes observed:

"When the facts change, I change my mind. What do you do?"

Panicking isn't ideal, but if you are going to do it, then do so early in the process.

The traditional student essay crisis approach does not work well in business.

Doing too little for too long and then bursting into random or poorly directed activity is not effective.

Too many briefs and tasks sit in in-trays until they become fiendishly difficult to answer or solve.

So next time you have a complex task, be sure to panic early.

Gather all the personnel that matter within the first 24 hours, generate an approach, and set it in motion.

You can always adjust later.

And for those who say they work better under pressure: you don't.

AXE
ADMINISTRIVIA

Most business people and companies have far too much to do.

Or at least it appears that way. But much of what they are doing could be described as 'administrivia'.

The more tasks we are given, the more important it becomes to work out what is truly worth doing, and what is not.

Most status reports and activity sheets have far too much on them.

This may make individuals and companies feel that they are being diligent.

But in truth it is more likely to be blurring their view of what really matters.

Concentrate on action, not activity.

Cull as many projects and tasks as possible.

Often, one single action can utterly transform a project or task.

Take the time to work out what that specific single action is, and just do that.

The amount of things that a company or an individual does is irrelevant.

No one ever said: "What a great project that was – it took over 500 meetings to get it done."

It's the outcome that matters, not the output.

So the question is not: "How much can we get done?"

The question is: "What is the easiest way to achieve our desired outcome?"

At the beginning of every project or task, put the emphasis on this question.

If you spend proper time doing that, then the rest will follow naturally.

And the outcome will arrive faster.

An Anti List is a list of things that you are *not* going to do.

This is a crucial aid in establishing what you *are* going to do.

Such a list establishes:

What you will *never* do.

What you don't *want* to do.

What you won't be doing in the near future.

All three perspectives are important in determining where growth will come from.

The first sets up principles to which the company can adhere.

The second flushes out desire and motivation.

The third determines priority.

Match the Anti List to the conventional task list and you have a powerful formula to provide your business with a clear centre of gravity for the coming year.

PART TWO

THINKING

GROWTH

COMMUNICATION

RELATIONSHIPS

CREATIVITY

INNOVATION

There is no point in talking unless you have point.

Too many people are, literally, pointless.

But it doesn't stop them talking.

Despite having no point, no point of view, and no line of argument, they start talking.

According to Princeton professor Harry G. Frankfurt, "Bullshit is stimulated whenever a person's obligations or opportunities to speak about some topic exceed their knowledge of the facts that are relevant to the topic."

In other words, they don't know what they are talking about.

Contrary to popular business belief, it's perfectly fine to say: "I don't know."

So, next time you are inclined to speak on a topic, make sure you have a genuine point.

When A.G. Lafley returned as Chief Executive of Procter & Gamble for the second time, he was appalled to find that most of the meetings he attended contained over 20 people.

He set about changing them in three ways.

No presentations were allowed (only a discussion of strategic issues agreed in advance), a maximum of five people in the room, and no more than three pages of new material in response to queries.

He also introduced a new discussion style called assertive inquiry, which blends advocacy (what I think) with inquiry (listen properly).

This is best summarized in the sentence:

"I have a view worth hearing, but I may be missing something."

This approach encourages well-informed confidence, but stops short of overconfidence.

And it encourages teamwork by requiring people to listen to the views of their colleagues.

So the right attitude is to blend opinion with inquiry.

Generating things to do makes companies feel productive, but many tasks may not be worth doing.

Projects often take on a life of their own.

A lot of people rush around but no one has stopped to ask one of the most important questions of all: *Do we really need to do this?*

This question is not cynical, nor is it an attempt to avoid work.

It is a vital line of inquiry to find out if what is being done has a clear purpose.

The upshot of not pausing to ask is that teams, and even whole companies, can slip into a groove of 'doing' rather than thinking.

And that doing eventually becomes "the way we do things round here."

Which could be a very dangerous thing.

As the comedy character Alan B'Stard famously observed: "Bollocks today - policy tomorrow."

Companies are full of people who bullshit,
but they are not necessarily liars.

They are phony rather than false.

They are faking things, but that doesn't necessarily
mean they get things wrong.

The bullshitter has much more freedom than
someone who tells the truth or lies, because they
do not require an anchor point on one side
or the other.

This does not mean rejecting the authority
of truth, as the liar does, or even opposing it.

It means paying no attention to it at all.

In the bullshit vortex, entire teams and companies
can spend thousands of hours just picking out
material, or making it up, to suit their purpose.

In amongst all this, they are not necessarily
getting anywhere.

If this is happening in your company,
it's time to ban the bull.

Ask anyone whether there are any wafflers
in their company and many will say yes.

Some confess to doing it themselves.

Most do it because they have an unformulated
idea taking shape in their head that they cannot
articulate in the spoken word.

Others do it when asked a question, and simply
start talking regardless of whether they have
anything helpful to say.

In some companies, this process repeats itself
all day and contributes to an unproductive
working environment.

This needs to stop.

For every waffler, there is a wafflee — someone
who has to listen to this drivel.

Wafflers need to rein it in. Instead of springing
a spontaneous word dump on someone, ask them:

"I have a roughly formulated idea I'd like
to discuss with you for five minutes. When
is convenient for you?"

TRICKLE OF DOUBT V. FLOOD OF NAKED TRUTH

Telling the truth makes your life easier.

For a start, you don't ever have to remember what you said, because you never lied.

Companies do too much lying.

Liars are unpleasant to be around.

And yet delivering news straight can be fraught too.

As Noel Coward said:

"It's discouraging to think how many people are shocked by honesty and how few by deceit."

When it comes to keeping people informed, you are better off replacing a trickle of doubt with a flood of naked truth.

Because, as historian C. Northcote Parkinson observed:

"The void created by the failure to communicate is soon filled with poison, drivel and misrepresentation."

THE POWER OF SEQUENCE

The animation company Pixar, creators of *Finding Nemo* and *Toy Story*, has a proven formula for successful storytelling.

What has become known as the Pixar Pitch involves six sequential sentences:

Once upon a time, A.

Every day, B.

One day, C.

Because of that, D.

Because of that, E.

Until finally, F.

All successful communication blends this kind of appeal with flexibility.

Getting the order right is critical for clear explanation.

And the power of the sequence ensures that your audience comes along with you.

DON'T ASSUME
PEOPLE WON'T
UNDERSTAND

"It's not what you say, it's what people hear."

So said American political pollster Frank Luntz.

And he's right.

This works in two directions.

First, almost everything anyone says can be completely misunderstood.

When you are communicating something, bear this in mind, especially if you are addressing a large audience.

Secondly though, do not patronize your audience by assuming they won't get it. They probably will.

If your message involves some complex technical detail, don't fudge or gloss over it.

Instead find an engaging way to explain it.

It's your job to ensure clear comprehension.

FIRST QUESTION, BIG PAUSE

The author and journalist Rebecca West famously asserted: "There is no such thing as conversation. It is an illusion. There are intersecting monologues, that is all."

Let's assume we are not all as cynical as her.

Conversation is not a monologue. It's two-way.

So it's a deal of sorts. You make yourself understood.

Then you pay attention carefully to what the other person is saying.

You assimilate that response, and then you adjust your next remarks accordingly.

Many people become flustered by this. They just keep on transmitting.

But remember, the other person is waiting for your response.

So instead of diving in with any old rubbish just to fill the silence, try leaving a big pause.

They have to wait because they asked a question. And you get time to think and say something thoughtful.

In the Jazz Café music venue in London, there are four letters painted onto a pillar by the stage.

STFU.

That means Shut The F*#k Up.

So the artistes can be heard properly.

You might think that's just jazz musicians for you.

But even the philosopher Simone Weil said:

"Attention is the rarest and purest form of generosity."

So if you really want to help out a colleague, give them your time and proper attention.

PART THREE

THINKING

GROWTH

RELATIONSHIPS

COMMUNICATION

CREATIVITY

INNOVATION

BE RELENTLESSLY CURIOUS

A lot of people think that those who come up with inspired ideas are either supremely talented or just plain lucky.

Neither is necessarily true, and it is possible to increase your chances of being innovative.

It all starts with being relentlessly curious.

You have to be intrinsically interested in a wide range of things.

Become a mental magpie, regularly picking up many stimuli.

When you have a tricky task or problem, you are effectively briefing your depth mind.

In due course, in what is sometimes called "The Unconcealing", your brain will attach an interesting observation to the task in hand.

That's not luck, nor plain serendipity.

It's a direct result of applying your curiosity to an issue.

That's how innovations emerge.

CLOSE
OR
FAR AWAY?

In the comedy programme of the same name, Father Ted tries in vain to explain to his hapless assistant the apparent size difference between objects (in this case a cow) that are close and far away.

"The Adjacent Possible" was a phrase coined by scientist Stuart Kauffman.

It refers to the nearest next steps that can be made in relation to any challenge.

It is always the best place to start when trying to innovate.

Far too many innovation challenges veer off into strange areas that are either impossible or undesirable to enact.

So begin the process by mapping out the elements closest to the subject.

Then work out the simplest next thing to do to expand outward from the centre.

Finding an opportunity that is close is always easier than one that is far away.

It's hard to move on when you, or a colleague, keep referring back to the past.

What happened before is only of passing interest.

Much more important is what is happening now or in the future.

So when it comes to generating new ideas, you need to forget the past.

As strategist and writer Adam Morgan says: "Break with your immediate past."

Or, put another way, forget everything you know and think again.

This approach is good for sweeping away the cobwebs of old thinking to allow a truly unfettered basis for fresh thinking.

It can also be a very useful rule in any idea generation or brainstorm session.

Nothing is perfect, and yet any meeting or company will almost certainly include some people who claim to be perfectionists.

Some perfectionists are defensive, and say they do it because no one else has standards as high as theirs.

But most perfectionists usually say that they do not like being that way, but can't help it.

Subordinates dread having a perfectionist boss, because nothing is ever good enough for them (apparently).

Their work is usually altered by their boss, so they often give up trying.

Perfectionists put additional pressure on their colleagues by taking far longer to complete work, with faster staff usually picking up the slack.

So, what to do?

Go for progress, not perfection.

Give it your best shot and then make it happen.

Planning is often a mirage.

There's nothing wrong with having a finely crafted Plan A, but the chances of it happening in precisely that fashion are low.

So you need a Plan B.

And quite possibly a Plan C, D, E, and so on.

Some people, and companies, become very frustrated when Plan A turns out to be ineffective.

This is usually because they have a high level of emotional investment in it.

But that is a poorly informed approach.

Because if Plan A is shown to be flawed, then there is no point in carrying on with it.

And the good news is that Plan B may well turn out to be *better* than Plan A.

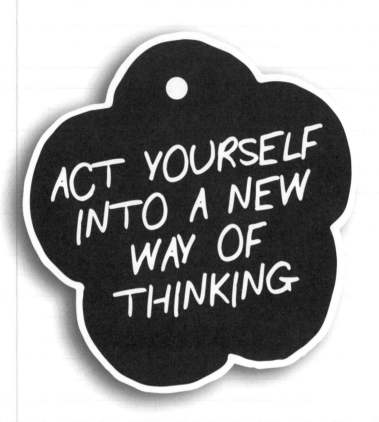

ACT YOURSELF
INTO A NEW
WAY OF
THINKING

People love sitting around talking about strategy.

It gives them an excuse to drink coffee and eat biscuits on company time.

But strategy is just a grand sounding word for what you have decided to do.

Unless you get on and do it, you're just talking.

Old academic joke: "Yes it works in practice, but does it work in theory?"

So, if your team or company spends too much time talking and not enough time doing, then they could do worse than heed this observation from business writer Richard Pascale.

"People are much more likely to act their way into a new way of thinking than think their way into a new way of acting."

In other words, once the thinking is done, stop talking and get on with it.

Then you'll really know if it works in practice.

PROTOTYPING
AS
SHORTHAND

Anyone can sit in a room and say
"Wouldn't it be great if...?"

To which the reasonable answer is: "Yes it would.
Can you make it work?"

This is where many a so-called brilliant idea
comes unstuck.

And it hasn't even reached the drawing board.

Making rough prototypes of proposed products cuts
to the chase fast and can avoid months or even
years of talk.

If it's a physical product, construct a rough working
version to show how it will work.

You will soon find out if it has merit.

If it's a service idea, then act it out to see if it works.

This is called 'bodystorming': using physical actions
to bring an idea in a brainstorm to life.

Fast and early prototyping improves any
innovation process.

Speed kills, or so the saying goes.

No it doesn't, at least according to
Jeremy Clarkson.

"Speed never killed anyone. Suddenly becoming
stationary, that's what gets you."

All projects benefit from momentum.

It's human nature.

We start off very excited with our new toy.

And then we have a motivational dip.

You can even plot the likely energy and enthusiasm
curve of a project before it starts.

So don't hang around letting bureaucracy and
inertia set in.

Grasp the initial energy of the new idea and
run with it as fast as possible.

And you'll know if it's a winner sooner than
if you let it lag.

RTFM. It stands for Read The F*@#king Manual.

This priceless acronym was the invention of exasperated engineers when trying to help clueless operators.

Those operators were invariably asking inane questions about how the product in question worked.

But they hadn't had the diligence to read the manual first.

If they had, then they would have had a better chance of knowing what they were doing.

Far too many people, and companies, try to wing it.

They pretty much make it up as they go along.

Occasionally it works, but usually it doesn't.

It's at this point that RTFM is extremely good advice.

Follow the process. Get trained properly.

Learn the details of the item in question.

Then proceed from a position of knowledge rather than ignorance.

FOOL'S GOLD
WHITE
SPACE

Fool's gold looks like gold, but it isn't.

It's usually some other yellow mineral like pyrite or chalcopyrite.

White space is blank, and when it's on a strategist's market map, it makes them think there's a gap to be exploited.

But they might be wrong, particularly when it comes to innovations.

'Fool's gold white space' is an apparent gap in the market, but in truth it's a failure masquerading as a viable opportunity.

Many an innovator has been fooled by it.

So next time you come across what appears to be an unoccupied area, ask yourself two questions.

Why is this space unoccupied?

What do they know that we don't?

PART FOUR

Creativity needs a decent place to flourish.

And yet many offices are sterile environments.

Air conditioning. Poor light, or no natural light.
Airless basements.

This is no place to be inventive, let alone
hold a brainstorm.

Research shows that people have more ideas when
the ceiling is high and if the walls are painted blue.

It reminds them of unfettered nature —
a world with no boundaries.

As the famous explorer Thor Heyerdahl
once remarked:

"Borders? I have never seen one. But I have
heard they exist in the minds of some people."

So if you crave creativity, create an
environment to help.

And that means a greenhouse where ideas
can grow and be nurtured.

The fuzzy front end is a phrase often used to describe the messy uncertain bit at the beginning of any project.

At this stage it may not be particularly evident how things are going to progress, or how it's all going to come together.

Don't panic. It's normal in any creative endeavour.

In fact, as business author Max McKeown points out:

"The fuzziness never really leaves as long as you are attempting to do something new."

In fact, he argues, there's often a fuzzy middle bit and a fuzzy back end as well.

So relax into it.

The best creative cultures and individuals are comfortable with ambiguity.

As Aristotle noted:

"It is the mark of an educated mind to be able to entertain a thought without accepting it."

All creativity involves some form of shot in the dark.

Discovery consists of seeing what everyone has seen and thinking what nobody has thought.

A leap from A to B, often via a somewhat unexpected C.

Small, incremental development of something that is already well established usually fails to provide sufficient differentiation.

So an element of destruction is needed.

Start by utterly 'destroying' the current version, solution, product, or whatever it is you are grappling with.

Clear the decks and try starting again.

Approach the challenge from two very different directions.

What *do* I know about it?

What *don't* I know about it?

Somewhere in the answers to those two questions lies a new originality.

It is fashionable to regard having lots of ideas as an indicator of a healthy business.

But it's not necessarily the number of ideas that matters.

It's how good they are.

And whether they ever get done.

In many cases, concentrating on too many ideas spreads resources too thinly.

And that can be as detrimental to success as not having many ideas at all.

So, don't just get rid of the bad ideas.

Kill some good ones as well.

Especially if they are not quite good enough.

This will leave all the available resource free to concentrate on those that have the potential to be truly great.

Sometimes quantity is the first step when generating creative ideas.

Out of a large volume of suggestions comes something workable and better.

If that's the case, then the language used in creative conversations can have a deep bearing on whether you and your team are likely to get anywhere.

Roger Martin, one of the great innovation and design thinkers of recent times, expressed this as:

"Managers need to take Ors and turn them into Ands."

In other words, instead of saying, "We could do this or this," the discussion should concentrate on "We could do this *and* this."

This is of course the opposite view to killing many ideas and just ending up with a few.

But it is interesting to note that the majority of the great companies with a reputation for creativity and innovation (such as Virgin and Procter & Gamble) tried many things first and just kept the winners.

When it comes to creativity, so called 'Aha'
or 'Eureka' moments are extremely unusual.

According to Steven Johnson, best selling author
of 'Where Good Ideas Come From', most great
ideas start with a hunch and slowly develop.

It all starts when you 'brief yourself'.

This is you telling your depth mind, or
sub-conscious, what the task in hand is.

Don't expect fireworks immediately.

And don't labour over it too much; the
harder you think, the worse it can get.

If you write down the rough idea, it is more likely to
emerge as a breakthrough later.

Probably when you are doing something
different entirely, which is why so many
people have excellent ideas when they are
in the shower, jogging, or painting a wall.

Have confidence in the slow hunch.

Everybody loves new stuff.

For some reason, it's usually more interesting than the old stuff.

But companies need to beware of novelty overload.

New ideas fight for attention, time and resources, and can prove very distracting if not properly channeled.

The knack is to pursue ruthless pruning of projects, and a healthy cynicism about the amount of time and resource a new idea will soak up.

"I had a monumental idea this morning, but I didn't like it."

So said Samuel Goldwyn, founder of the Metro-Goldwyn-Mayer film company.

It takes courage to recognize something for what it is, and then reject it if necessary in the interests of the greater good.

So, next time you or your team has an apparently brilliant idea, first consider rejecting it.

Sometimes, there is no point in carrying on.

In business, this thought can lend two helpful perspectives.

First, some people and companies simply don't want to give up what they have had up till now.

This may be the right thing to do, but where creativity is required, hanging on to old ways is rarely productive.

Second, when everyone has become far too committed to something that clearly isn't working, then pulling out can be the best option.

Although painful, quitting is better than persisting with something sub-standard.

Pulling the plug on any project requires bravery, particularly when everyone has invested so much time and effort.

But sometimes it's the right thing to do.

Martina Navratilova was described as "the greatest singles, doubles, and mixed doubles player who's ever lived."

That was some compliment, coming from former World Number One player Billie Jean King.

This is what Martina had to say about commitment:

"Other players are involved in tennis, but I'm committed. It's like ham and eggs. The chicken is involved; the pig is committed."

So there you have it. If you want to push creativity to the limit, you need to be fully committed.

There's no point in going into it half-hearted.

In fact, if you do find yourself losing enthusiasm, then you might reasonably conclude that the idea is not good enough.

So try harder.

A 'Done' Wall is something proposed by Scott Belsky in his book 'Making Ideas Happen'.

Done Walls are a highly motivating idea.

Put everything the team has done on the wall as massive checklists, thereby continually reminding everyone of how much progress has been made.

It makes the place look like a productivity factory, so no one sits around worrying that they are not getting anywhere.

Beware that there is a huge difference between these true steps of progress and other irrelevant stuff that has no real bearing on forward motion.

Procrastinators typically do far too much insecurity work — stuff with no intended outcome that is quick enough to do, without them (or anyone else) realizing that it's actually a waste of time.

So the Done Wall is the home of genuinely helpful pieces of progress that confirm to everyone that you are really getting somewhere.

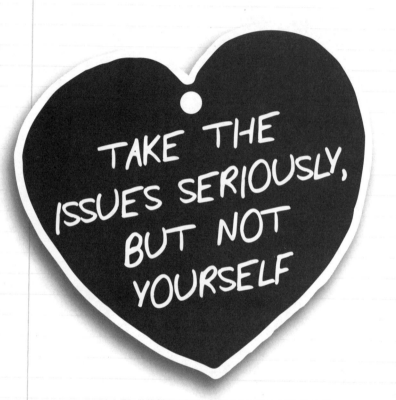

PART FIVE

TAKE THE
ISSUES SERIOUSLY,
BUT NOT
YOURSELF

"All jokes will be taken seriously."
Border crossing sign.

There are some really serious people around.

To them, everything is such a big deal.

Hubris. Self-aggrandizement. Arrogance. Pomposity.
Self-importance.

Call it what you like. But it doesn't have to
be this way.

It's perfectly possible to approach issues seriously
whilst still adopting a light touch to personalities
and people.

A little self-deprecation goes a long way.

We don't all have to be gun slinging, brash,
world-beating executives.

In fact, none of us should be really.

So when it comes to work, take the issues
seriously, but not yourself.

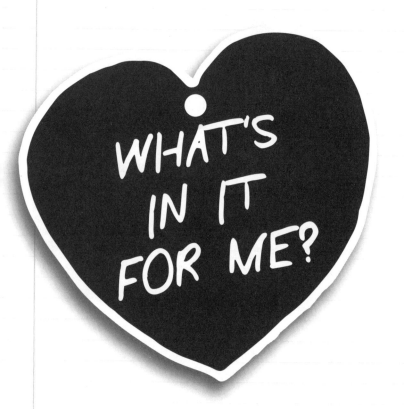

WHAT'S
IN IT
FOR ME?

This simple question works in two very different directions.

Both are highly poignant.

First, directed inward to yourself: 'What's in it for me?'

This is a critical way to work out whether you want to do something or not.

If you see no satisfaction in the task or project, then try to avoid it.

Second, put yourself in the shoes of the other person, and imagine them asking: 'What's in it for me?'

If you cannot generate a satisfactory answer on their behalf, then the other person is unlikely to agree with you, or be satisfied with what you are asking them to do.

People have to be sufficiently motivated in order to agree with you or perform well.

It might be a financial point, but more often it is simply a matter of motivation.

The French philosopher Simone Weil said:
"Humility is attentive patience."

Humility goes a long way.

And yet many managers are strident, hectoring, macho, and domineering.

It's not good enough.

It's completely unnecessary. And it's not even an effective technique.

You might think that there are benefits to this approach, but there are none.

So, companies should be in search of managers with modesty. People who don't have to show off regularly.

Or brag incessantly.

Or always take the credit.

So if you are hiring, look for modesty.

And if you are managing people, show some humility and spread the joy a bit.

Working out likely cause and effect only takes a few seconds.

Consider for a moment: "If I do x, then y will (almost certainly) happen."

You can then analyze whether y is desirable or not, before you act.

If y is desirable, then do x.

If y is irrelevant or inconsequential, then still do x.

If y is not desirable, then don't do x.

This last one is arguably the hardest.

Too many people do things that will clearly have undesired consequences, but they still do them anyway.

Pausing to think for just a few seconds can remove thousands of instances of this happening.

A broad church has lots of different types of people in it.

Variety is not only welcomed, but actively encouraged.

So when you are putting teams together, do not hire in your own image.

You will simply end up with lots of mini versions of you.

Doubtless they will have all your talents and traits, but also all your faults and deficiencies.

"Hire character. Train skill." So said Peter Schutz, the Chief Executive of Porsche.

Be open-minded about different styles, and embrace them to create a richly diverse team.

Then allocate the right tasks to the right people.

You can't ask nine women to make a baby in a month.

Dividing up work arbitrarily doesn't necessarily mean faster and better results.

You need the right people doing the right stuff.

Polar explorer Roald Amundsen beat Captain Scott to the South Pole by consistently marching 20 miles a day.

He had worked out in advance that 20 miles was the optimum amount for a team with their equipment.

In bad weather the team did it anyway, and in good they stopped at 20 to save energy for the next day.

Scott's team either stayed in their tents on bad days or overshot on good ones and wore themselves out.

The moral is that companies, teams and individuals should aim for similar consistency.

This is what the business authors Collins and Hansen call 'fanatic discipline'.

Don't ease off just because things are difficult, or overdo it when things are easy.

Apply consistent 20 mile marches, and ask the same of your colleagues.

It seems the world is obsessed with everything being BIG. Old joke:

Texan: "Where I come from boy, I can drive all day and still be on my own land."

Englishman: "Yeah, I had a car like that once."

Big doesn't necessarily mean good. It could even be bad.

By contrast, there are tremendous advantages to making small changes.

Behavioural science has shown that tiny variations in phraseology can cause huge change.

Small changes are usually less costly, and often free.

Small changes attract less attention from bosses and meddlers, so they are easier to implement.

Small changes are easier to rectify if they don't achieve their original objective.

So bear in mind that the 'next big thing' could be small.

Being personable costs nothing and makes
your working life more pleasant.

It also makes it better for everyone else.

Constructive, thoughtful people attract more
of the same.

They give and earn respect.

Which means a calmer, less stressed
working environment.

Part of the knack is always having time to help
out a colleague.

So when they ask if you have a minute to discuss
something, the answer should, within reason, be yes.

This level of respect and attentiveness also allows
you to be candid without being brusque.

As actress and comedian Amy Poehler says:

"If you can speak about what you care about
to a person you disagree with without denigrating
them, then you may actually be heard."

That's good news for everybody.

Ever been to an important meeting where someone (often the most senior person) failed to turn up?

The meeting proceeds, and the people who did have the courtesy to turn up agree something productive and useful.

Some time later, the senior person who wasn't there overrules or ignores the recommendation that the team has made.

This is not on.

No show = no say.

In other words, if you can't be bothered to turn up, then you forfeit your right to contribute, let alone exert a power of veto.

Senior managers need to heed this.

Breathlessly lurching from meeting to meeting poorly briefed and under prepared, or failing to make it at all, is dysfunctional behaviour.

Even worse, if you never made the meeting at all, then at least respect your people by letting them get on with it.

There's a Meat Loaf song called 'Everything Louder Than Everything Else'.

This is roughly how many people operate in business, especially frenetic bosses.

They want full throttle on everything.

They initiate too many projects.

They want their staff working all hours on all fronts.

They don't set a single objective. They set multiple ones.

And they want it all now, or possibly even yesterday.

This leaves everyone confused, and incapable of knowing what to deal with next.

Setting clear priorities is critical.

Be ruthless on tasks, remove low priority items, and set people running on one thing at a time.